NORTHERN KENT

Edited by Carl Golder

GW00693931

First published in Great Britain in 1998 by
POETRY NOW YOUNG WRITERS
1-2 Wainman Road, Woodston,
Peterborough, PE2 7BU
Telephone (01733) 230748

HB ISBN 0 75430 187 7
SB ISBN 0 75430 188 5

FOREWORD

With over 63,000 entries for this year's Cosmic competition, it has proved to be our most demanding editing year to date.

We were, however, helped immensely by the fantastic standard of entries we received, and, on behalf of the Young Writers team, thank you.

The Cosmic series is a tremendous reflection on the writing abilities of 8-11 year old children, and the teachers who have encouraged them must take a great deal of credit.

We hope that you enjoy reading *Cosmic Northern Kent* and that you are impressed with the variety of poems and style with which they are written, giving an insight into the minds of young children and what they think about the world today.

CONTENTS

Palm Bay CP School

Sarah Wreford	49
Oliver Harris	49
Adam Heather	50
Kelly Thorn	51
Hollie Dixon	51
Sarah Pryor	52
Emma Wallace	52
Stephanie Hackworth	52
Matthew Kelly	53
Lee Huddleston	53
Carlie Pearlman	53
Rebecca Huckstep	54
Kieran Mannings	54
James Spear	55
Johnathan Fell	55
Richard Gray	56
Christopher Young	56
Tara Sutton	57
Alice Martin	57
Alexandra Pacey	58
Amy Quy-Verlander	58
Alex Grace	59
Luke Dyer	59
Phillip Alexandrakis	60
Hannah Dunn	60
Kirsty McChesney	61
Claire Tiley	61
Jadie Hards	62
Charlotte Tournay	62
Natalie Baughan	62
Philip Nesbit	63
Charlotte Ende	63

Karen Parish	79
Matthew Mole	80
Daniel Dowsing	81
Hannah Baker	82
Daniel Sperrin	82
Samantha Hewish	83
Steven Smith	83
Katie Hebditch	84
Laura Ray	84
Ben Manuel	85
Amy Warner	86
Natasha Risely	86
Megan Kelly	87
Ryan Joy	87
George Broom	88
Faye Andrew	88
Katie Dearden	89
Stephanie Coombes	89
Kirsty Logan	90
Amy Spray	90
Cara Nicholson	91
Stephanie Chaplin	91
Laura Dampier	92
Paul Saunders	92
Lucy Woolford	93
Jessica Read	93
Natasha Tiwari	94
Shelley Tapsell	94
Lucy Rees	95
Atina Ellis	95
Natalie Jane Read	96
Kimberley Platt	96
Laura Ellis	97
Jonathan Costello	98
Amanda Holmes	98
Michael Rose	99
Lauren Mason	100
Laura Knight	100

THE POEMS

THE PLACE WHERE THE SUN SHINES

The waves charge for the shore,
Splashing the people in their bathing suits,
Children screaming, swimming under the waves,
Until a big wave sucks them under.
Adults bathing in the hot air,
When it gets too hot they
Squeeze some more lotion on,
Trying to get a brown tan to show off.

The sun shining on the white grains of sand,
People digging their toes in the burning sand.
The ice-cream van plays its song,
Children rush to try and get there first,
Eating melting, runny, soft ice-cream
Letting it run down their chin.
While children build a big sand castle,
Rushing to and fro pouring more water into the moat.

The muscular life guard waiting on look-out point,
Listening for screams to save.
People wearing hats, glasses and bathing suits.
The palm trees swaying in the breeze,
Letting coconuts fall down,
A man shouting along the sea shore,
'Fresh spices! Buy your fresh spices!'
The smell of spices freshens up my mouth.

I do like to be where the sun shines!

Tara Cowland (11)
Convent Preparatory School

THE LIFE OF A HAMSTER

I am a hamster, my home is a cage,
My name is Sandy and I'm one year of age.
My territory extends to a house, a garden and tree
And a mummy, granny and grandie to take good care of me.

The only thing to complain about
Is the fact that they always clean me out
When I've spent every day and night
Making my bed just right.

Mummy comes along each fateful Sunday,
And throws my precious bed away.
Yes, every week they clean me out
I stamp my paws and want to pout!

But Mummy buys me tasty seeds,
Nuts and fruit to fulfil my needs,
The tastiest of morsels to eat
Every imaginable sort of treat.

When it's not food she buys tunnels to run
And climbing things where I can have fun.
As you see there are advantages in having a mummy
Who gets a lot of pocket money!

The household cat, he stares at me,
Can't a hamster have any privacy?
I can't even use my corner without being seen,
By that annoying cat with eyesight so keen.
He's not exactly a threat,
He's a very lazy sort of pet.

But I'm very happy normally,
With lots of love from everybody.
I must stop writing now, you see,
I'm the sort of hamster that gets hungry!

Alexandra Kurt (11)
Convent Preparatory School

A LIONESS'S DAY

Waking up in the frosty morning,
I go outside looking for breakfast.
A herd of deer or a herd of zebra
I choose the deer. Yum!
I creep through the long, dried grass,
Every movement has to be soundless,
Otherwise breakfast will run away.
Oh no, tiger has beat me to it!
Tiger races after it with his long tail chasing him.
His fiery red fur and long lingering tail.
I'll have to go back to my lazy husband.

I lie down and relax in the scorching sun,
Watching two lions fighting, just for pleasure.
First they circle each other with menacing eyes,
Then they pounce I can see their gleaming white teeth,
Growling noises come from the back of their throats.
I lie back and look at the sky,
Trying to make pictures from the clouds,
I fall asleep and dream of fantasy land,
I am a lioness lying by the beach,
Sipping my fruit juice, trying to get a tan,
I wake up and the two lions have crept away,
I will get them for this!

Claire Shirley (11)
Convent Preparatory School

MY HOLIDAY

I'm going on holiday,
It will be such fun,
Playing in the pools,
With bouncy balls.

Having lots of races,
Splashing in the pool.
Then we'll have another ice-cream,
To cool us right down.

It's soon time to get ready
To go out for a meal,
We'll have a lot to eat,
Then sit down by the pool.

I'll be very tired after our long day,
So I'll jump into my bed.
With a very big thought
Of what tomorrow brings.

But then I realise,
I still have to wait,
Four days until the day,
I fly away.

Amy Calnon (10)
Convent Preparatory School

THE SUN

The sun is like the eye of heaven,
That is beaming down on us,
The sun is the break of day,
Shining like a blistering fire.

Warm yellow and orange,
Are the sun's colours,
Mingled together as the sun burns
Ferociously from its furnace.

Gemma Watkins (11)
Convent Preparatory School

THE GOAL

Pass, I shouted as I stood in the middle of a green pool,
Surrounded by a sea of red and white,
Fans amazed at my team's ability and skill,
I shouted pass again.

Now the ball comes closer and closer,
High in the air over many,
It lands at my feet and as if by magic,
It sticks to them and I take it further up the field.

I feel like the finest person in the world,
As the wind brushes against my face,
And defenders are left standing helplessly,
As if stranded on a desert island.

Now I see the corner of the net,
Then the energy and speed are let out,
My leg is lifted back and hits the ball,
Which was quite painful I must admit.

The ball soars through the air,
Everyone gazes in astonishment,
The ball hits the back of the net,
So the celebrations begin.

David Winstone (10)
Convent Preparatory School

THE SNOWMAN

There once was a chubby little snowman,
With a carrot nose,
With a scarf wrapped around his neck,
And a hat upon his head.

He stood at the back of the garden,
All lonely and sad,
Wondering whether anybody would come
Out and play.

Nobody did ever come to play with that poor snowman,
And so he gradually melted away,
And all that was left was a hat,
A scarf and a very flimsy carrot!

Abigail Sparks (10)
Convent Preparatory School

STREET LIFE

The moonlight flickers with glittering stars,
Planes seize the dark, gloomy, plain black sky.

It is a night of the full moon
And I wander down the sleepy highway,
With a few lamp posts here and there
To guide my way to nowhere.

I pass a silent, calm lake
Which reflects my sizeless figure.
Wobbling like a jelly,
As a sudden breeze shatters the glass.

The brume-frosty air fills my lungs,
As I fall asleep mutely upon a wooden bench.

Mark Ferrill (10)
Convent Preparatory School

UNDERNEATH THE SEA

Underneath the sea, the seaweed
Sways from side to side.

Underneath the sea the fish search the
Mystical world of the sea, searching for food.

Underneath the sea the yellow and brown sand
Looks like gold sparkling in the water.

Underneath the sea the star fish
Look like red stars sparkling upon a rock.

Underneath the sea like a torch
Lighting up the sea.

Underneath the sea, the sea is like
A whole new world waiting to be discovered.

Natasha Brennan (11)
Convent Preparatory School

BLUE AND GREEN

Have you ever seen such blue,
That pierces through,
Have you ever seen such green,
That shines through every speck of dew
Out in the dark forest.
Have you ever seen such blue
That pierces through.
Have you ever seen such green in every
                    speck of dew.
It shines beautifully like a glimmering emerald,
And the blue shimmering like a sapphire.

Maxine Buchanan (10)
Convent Preparatory School

TIGER

I can remember running free,
With nothing to worry me.
A sharp crack of a twig,
I wonder what it is.

Stalkers! With their guns poised,
And nets ready, looking for me.
I make a quick run for it,
My slender body shivering with fear.

A quick speed up to taller grass,
Suddenly a sharp pain in my back.
They caught me with a single shot,
I gradually fall to sleep.

I'm put on a ship, what to do?
Put in a cage all alone,
In a place called a zoo,
People all around me.

'Wow! Look at that,' they all say,
As I walk from corner to corner.
I really do miss my old home,
Running free among the grass.

It is time they throw my food into the cage,
But sometimes it is hidden from me.
It does not taste like my normal food,
I am stuck here forever more.

Caroline Savin (10)
Convent Preparatory School

NIGHT-TIME

Night-time is a dreamy time,
When nocturnal animals hunt for food,
Where the dark streets are lit up by orange lights,
And alleyways are left for dead.
Strange people lurk in the shadows,
Sane people sleep in bed.

Night-time is a quiet time,
Owls hoot and bats fly.
Most people lay asleep,
They prefer to be indoors,
Lights are off and snoring is on,
We all are feeling sleepy.

Night-time is a scary time,
Some people are afraid of night,
You cannot see much without light,
Strange things come out at night,
Like birds and huge insects,
Flying and crawling straight at you.

Night-time is a cold time,
In hot countries it is below freezing,
Because of the clouds,
No wonder we all are asleep,
Otherwise we would get frostbite!
I hate night-time.

Roy Nada (11)
Convent Preparatory School

A Rugby Match

Gum shield in,
Scrum cap on,
Pull my sleeves up,
And win the mighty battle.

The match starts and I go roaring on,
As I am no friend to my opposition.
I tackle him, he goes head first in the mud,
I give no sympathy.

I get up, I go running on,
Then the referee called a scrum,
My father yelled, 'Big push.'
We pushed fiercely and won the ball.

The ball goes out and we decide to kick it,
Then from the touch line I hear, 'Run for it.'
But they catch it.
Someone tackles him, the ball comes loose.

We pick the ball up and pass it to me.
I go and score a try
Everyone is jumping up and down joyfully.

James Newman (10)
Convent Preparatory School

The Ocean

The ocean is like a big blue blanket,
Dolphins, whales, jellyfish and tropical fish swim around
In the deep blue ocean and they get their food from seaweed.

You can get coral in different shapes and sizes,
I like the different colours underneath the ocean,
It is really amazing,
Underneath the ocean the fish are searching for food.

The ocean is very deep and wonderful,
The ocean is full of different colours,
The ocean is full of excitement,
The ocean is a wonderful place.

Charlotte House (10)
Convent Preparatory School

GOING TO THE FOOTBALL MATCH

Click go the turnstiles as I go through the gate,
Coke in hand I find my seat,
Then the players come out of the tunnel.
A pang of excitement rushes through all of me.

England take the centre,
The crowd cheer encouragingly all around me.
Then Shearer passes to Gascoigne,
Alleluia, at last England score a goal!

One - nil, one - nil, the football fans shout,
And the referee blows the half-time whistle.
I go off to get a hot sausage roll,
I come back too late. Oh no they've scored a goal!

The Colombian fouled Southgate,
Southgate goes off with a sprained ankle and the Colombian gets a
                                                            red card.
The game goes into injury time and England get a corner,
Beckham curls it round the post into the goal.

I walk home through the twin towers triumphant,
Down the steps to the crowded tube station.
I get in the tube, I don't have to hold on it's so crowded.
I get home and flop down on a chair, thinking about the victory.

Thomas Gosnell (10)
Convent Preparatory School

MY DREAM SHOP

My ideal shop would be,
A shop with sweets all for free
They would have all you need
Even flower seed.

It would be where famous people shopped,
And even a dog called Lucy Lopped.
Not forgetting all the road,
They would go and come back with a load.

It would be my own creation,
I would call it *My Sensation*
People would come from near and far
Just to try out the shop Spar.

Phone this number and
Entertainment you will get
It will amuse your pet
By following the shop going down the street
Looking for tasty things to eat.

Tel: 459970.

Sophie Messam (11)
Convent Preparatory School

THE COLOUR OF THE SKY

As the sun sets over the rippling sea,
Colours of red, yellow and orange mingle together
And light up for the newly dawned night.

People lie on the soft gentle sand
Seeping in the last few rays of the sun
Clouds float gently across the sky
They have changed to soft purple.

People have left,
The sun has gone down,
Silence is dawning for miles around.
The sky has darkened to a midnight blue
The moon's now appeared
Dancing along in its yellow glow.

Georgina Jansz (10)
Convent Preparatory School

GREEN

Today everything is green
My dad's face,
My mum's vase
Everything is green
I wonder what has happened?

As I wander through the house
I notice everything is green
The television is so green
I must be on an alien wavelength.

Just then I knocked something green
Mum's vase has smashed
Green bits of crockery
Lie pathetically all around.

Mum rushes in
'My vase!' she shouts.
'Gordon, you've ruined my glasses they're green!'

I just answer with a sickly green smile
Then realise everything is changing in slow motion.
Changing in slow motion back to the many colours of human earth.
I land back with a thud.

Gordon Thomson (11)
Convent Preparatory School

NOISES

When I'm in bed I can hear the gusty wind thudding on my window,
In the park I can hear the ducks quacking with a triumphant sound,
But the most fierce noise is when I'm in the zoo when the great lions
are roaring,
And that can make your eardrums explode.

My next door neighbours fight like cat and dog and that is not a
pleasant sound.
When a dog is chasing a cat you can hear the cat screaming wildly
at the sight of the dog.
The mouse's little, running feet sound like tapping of rain on the
window.
But the noise of snow drops slashing on to the ground is a great
experience.

At a concert the music is so beautiful that it is a very pleasant sound,
A drumming noise is like a heart beating fast,
The sweet playing of a violin is as merry as singing a Christmas song,
But the amazing noise of an orchestra is an unbelievable sound.

The wonderful songs of Christmas are enjoyable,
The wonderful excitement of playing an instrument is unbelievable.
When people are dancing to music that they love it is enjoyed all over
the world,
That's why sometimes noises are wonderful.

Dharmendra Toor (10)
Convent Preparatory School

THE SUN

As the sun rises into the sky,
Cockerels cry out a new day is dawning
Its light shines on the earth,
Making the other part of the world die.

As its light grows brighter
It rises to the top of the sky,
Its golden beams strike down
Reaching over the land.

The sky shines with its dark blue
And the pale white clouds,
In all shapes blocking the sun
Yet it still peeps through
Making the sky look like heaven.

As the time goes by
The sun begins to set,
And night begins to descend
The stars are coming out
And shining real bright too!

The sun is departed
And its rays have gone,
It's all right, tomorrow will be another day
For the bright yellow sun.

Michael Horwood (10)
Convent Preparatory School

The Bully

He follows me everywhere
Every single day,
He punches me and pulls my long blonde hair,
In a horrible sort of way,
He'll make me do his homework,
Or will give me a violent threat,
But what I hate most of all,
He'll treat others like a pet,
Tonight I'll be going home with a black eye,
And I suppose my mum will wonder why,
But this time I can't deny.
'It's the *bully*,' I shout with a rather loud voice.
'And you didn't tell me before.
You're an idiot,' my mum screams.
I'm usually used to Mum's scream
But this time I can't ignore
They way she felt, so sore.

Yasmin Barnard (11)
Convent Preparatory School

The Game

As soon as we rush out of the tunnel,
There is excitement all around,
The tempo is high,
The supporters are in tune,
And everyone is ready to do battle.

I get the ball and momentarily
Pass to my team mate who was calling for it.
Everyone watches in amazement as he tries a shot from far out.

No one moves except the opposing goalkeeper
Who stretches for the ball,
But his effort to prevent us from scoring was nothing
As the ball sailed into the top right hand corner,
We scored! Jubilation among the fans.

It was the end of the match,
Final score 1-0 to us
As we walked back to the changing rooms satisfied with a win,
The sweet smell of victory is waiting for us all back at home.

Daniel Laffan (11)
Convent Preparatory School

PEOPLE

While I stroll down the long street
So many folk I observe.
Some jubilant,
Others in the blues,
However none similar to me.

My eyes dart here and there,
And of all the things surrounding me,
They are mostly people.
In the most bizarre costumes.
However none dressed similar to me.

While pacing through the alley,
I see two people alike,
In every possible way,
I would love a twin,
I must seek one identical to me.

Katherine O'Connor (10)
Convent Preparatory School

What The World Means To Me

I see the world from my point of view,
As a place of excitement and hope,
As a place where the tiniest things can grow,
That's what the world means to me.

I see the world from my point of view,
As a place of happiness, joy and love,
As a place where all people live,
That's what the world means to me.

I see the world from my point of view,
As a place where my life has begun,
As a place where my life also must end.
That's what the world means to me.

Alice Jones (11)
Convent Preparatory School

Our Earth

Lava flowing and rocks tumbling
Glowing stars and planets.
Star clusters and floating stars around.
The planet is green and blue with
Mountains as high as the moon.
Where the sun sets colours of red and orange appear,
And mammoth cliffs of coloured rock
Which jut out into the ocean
Hurled up from the sea bed
By titanic forces.
Our turbulent earth,
Held up by the creatures and people
Who live upon it.

James Scutts (11)
Convent Preparatory School

DEATH

As I lay in bed sweltering hot I begin
To think about a plot.
The lonely deserted land outside,
How did it begin and when will it die.

I sometimes wonder why, oh why
Do we have to die.
Surely the earth could bear it
If I stayed the troublesome child.

I walk along the sandy shore,
Listening for yells and roars of people crying to
                                          their death.
But here I am lying in bed
Don't worry child just rest your head.

Andrea Goodman (11)
Convent Preparatory School

MY TAMAGOTCHI

I've got a Tamagotchi I feed it every day.
I clean my Tamagotchi when it gets dirty.
It's doing well hooray!
Then it started bleeping when it got sleepy.
It really drove me mad.
So I asked my mum if I was allowed
To take out the batteries
My mum said, 'Yes! It's driving me mad.'
I did that
And now I really wish I'd never done it.

Hayley Tyrrell (9)
Grove Park CP School

ANIMALS

The tiger is a magnificent beast
from many large animals he makes his feast.
A monkey swings from branch to branch
and finds the fruit on which to munch.
The elephant stamps from place to place,
he's far too big to win a race.

Laura Wood (8)
Grove Park CP School

JULIE BAKER

I have a friend called Julie Baker,
she always dresses hippie.
She's got the greatest set of shoes,
and is greedy with the Matchmakers.

I have a friend called Julie Baker,
but I ask myself why?
I could have chosen Martie Ringlestone,
but she always was sly.

I've got a friend called Julie Baker,
she always smells real nice.
I saw her at the party,
but she was cold as ice.

I have a friend called Julie Baker,
and sure as you will see.
She comes around and plays,
and then goes home for tea.

Emma Wood (9)
Grove Park CP School

Roman Poem

Romans wore sandals to protect their feet
They ate chickens, pigs and all sorts of meat.

Romans wore armour when going to war
They used shields, swords, weapons many more.

They built roads, cities, towns and forts,
Castles, houses, theatres, all sorts.

Amber Lenton (8)
Grove Park CP School

Winter Snow

Snowballs flying
Crisp snow
Frozen ice
Cold winds blow.

People sledding
Wrapped up tight
It's getting dark
Now it is night.

As black as coal
So calm and still
All is quiet
Until . . .

The trees are dripping
Morning is here
There's a rising sun
To make the snow disappear.

Helena Dowsett (10)
Highfield Junior School

THE ASTRONAUT

There was a dumb astronaut
Who decided to go to the moon
But the thing about this astronaut
He flew in a helium balloon.

The day came when he
Had to do the task
He held on tight
And went up with a blast.

As he went up he
Passed the hot sun
Smelt something burning
But just carried on.

Eventually looked up
A hole was burning fast
He quietly said help
But then shouted out blast.

Next he's in the high street
People were gathering round
Holding on to his spacesuit
He ran right out of town.

Clare Lipscomb (10)
Highfield Junior School

THE MOON

There is a thing up in the sky
It's very big at night,
It's opposite the sun
But reflects it back so bright.

It's got deep holes called craters
Which men have gone to explore.
Now they want to go back
To see them more and more.

We all hoped there was life there
But now we've been proved wrong.
I was very disappointed
After waiting for so long.

I thought that it was made of cheese
And full of little green men.
With three legs and one huge eye,
But I was wrong again.

I would like to go to the moon
In a spaceship so colossal,
I would take my family with me
In the search to find a fossil.

Tim Chase (11)
Highfield Junior School

NONSENSE POEM

I had a friend called Russell
His middle name was Brussel
He had a big brain
And got stuck down a drain.

I had a friend called Mat
He looked rather fat
He saw a ginger cat
And whacked it with a bat.

I had a friend called Clare
She looked like a bear
She tore lots of ham
And looked like Spam.

I had a friend called Scott
He had lots of spots
He played a game called dots
And saw lots of pots.

I have a friend called Tim
I found him in a bin
He is very dim
And looks like Jim.

I had a friend called Jane
She came from Spain
She lived down the lane
And owned a crane.

Matthew Oliver (10)
Highfield Junior School

THE BULLY

There once was a big bully
In our very big school
He was cruel and mean
Tall and obscene
With a punch and a kick
His reactions were quick
He gave everyone a cut
With his big head-butt
He knocked them flat
With a baseball bat
He stood them on a bench
And hit them with a wrench
He tied their hair in a knot
And bashed them with a pot
But one amazing day he fell flat on his face
We thought it was brilliant, ace
So don't be mean or I'll be guessin'
You'll be learning a very good lesson
I'm sure you'll agree it isn't a joke
That people like us have to suffer these folk
But perhaps we can try and show some compassion
For these very sad folk who behave in this fashion.

Miles McGuire (11)
Highfield Junior School

CHOCOLATE!

Lots of chocolate is very
Yummy especially when
It's in your tummy.

Chocolates dark, milk and
White, different flavours
(out of sight)

It's hard and soft and can
be sticky, if you eat too
much it's very sickly.

It's rich and round, long
and tall and it can come
in the shape of a ball.
Chocolate . . . Neat stuff!

Emma Schultz (11)
Highfield Junior School

CHOCOLATE BOX

In my magic caramel sea,
I can hear the golden waves beating near me.

In my magic strawberry cream army,
I can see them eating chilli con carne.

In my magic walnut wizard,
I see him conjuring up a blizzard.

In my magic coffee land,
Cadbury's have just created a nutty brand.

In my magic coconut castles,
Bounties arrive in large brown parcels.

Michael Cowburn (11)
Lower Halstow Primary School

HANDS . . .

When I clap my disastrous hands loudly . . .
People fall over suddenly.

When I clap my disastrous hands loudly . . .
Windows noisily break.

When I clap my disastrous hands loudly . . .
Flash cars crash into each other.

When I clap my disastrous hands loudly . . .
A terrible earthquake arrives and it destroys everything.

I click my careful fingers quietly . . .
And everything goes back to normal.

I am so pleased, I clap loudly for joy,
Oh No!

Olivia Spree (10)
Lower Halstow Primary School

MY FRIEND

My friend, is always there when I need
someone to care.

My friend, never breaks a promise.

My friend, always shares thoughts and
ideas with me.

My friend *always* seems to make things
come alive.

My friend, is always kind and loyal to me.

I'm so lucky to have a friend like mine.

Marie Jacobs (10)
Lower Halstow Primary School

IN MY MAGIC DREAMLAND

In my magic dreamland
Tall dragons can dance
And great falls can sing.

In my magic dreamland
Great trees can talk and
Spectacular bushes can walk.

In my magic dreamland
Impressive rocks roll over
The vast plains that sweep the land.

In my magic dreamland
Large fish catch bears and
Roast them golden brown.

In my magic dreamland
Things turn into a caramel chocolate
From a soft ice-cream, yum, yum.

David Fordham (9)
Lower Halstow Primary School

WHEN I YAWN

When I yawn I suck up . . .
All the history books in the greeny-blue world,
Then I swallow them!

When I yawn I suck up . . .
All the colour TVs in the greeny-blue world,
Then I swallow them!

When I yawn I suck up . . .
All the cotton wool clouds in the greeny-blue world,
Then I swallow them!

When I yawn I suck up . . .
All the huge buildings in the greeny-blue world,
Then I swallow them!

When I yawn I suck up . . .
All the greeny-blue world
Then I burp!

Faye Smith (9)
Lower Halstow Primary School

THE STORM

When I clap my hands,
Leaves and twigs begin to rustle.

When I clap my hands,
Rain starts falling lightly, yes very lightly.

When I clap my hands,
I hear in the distance the sound of thunder.

When I clap my hands,
A flash of lightning appears in the sky.

When I clap my hands,
The rain gets heavier and bounces off the road.

When I clap my hands,
A crash of thunder deafens everyone.

When I clap my hands,
Hailstones fall from the sky.

When I clap my hands,
Lightning shines over everything.

When I clap my hands,
The storm is all over.

Ruth Walker-Grice (11)
Lower Halstow Primary School

UNDER MY CREEPY BED I HEAR

Under my creepy bed I hear
Slimy monsters speaking
About my horrible future.

Under my creepy bed I hear
Mice rustling around
Looking for mouldy cheese.

Under my creepy bed I hear
My death clock saying
'Die! Die! Die!'

Under my creepy bed I hear
Swift hurricanes
Destroying cities.

Under my creepy bed I hear
Thunder and lightning
Coming to attack me.

Under my creepy bed I hear
My ancient toys
Coming to life.

Under my creepy bed I hear
A nasty mob
Coming to raid my house.

Kaidee Sibborn (11)
Lower Halstow Primary School

MAGICAL FISH-BOWL

I stare into my magic fish-bowl
And with a flick of magic seaweed
I saw the castle clear and bright
A fair maiden let down her hair from a high window.
I saw a king frowning at a jester
Who made a sweet sound from
a horn.
Up in the hillside I saw Jack and Jill
falling down the hill.
I saw a lion in a corner with a sharp
thorn in his paw.
I stare even more . . .
I saw Miss Muffet sitting on a tuffet.
Then I blinked. It's only my magical fish-bowl.

Charlotte Low (9)
Lower Halstow Primary School

I WISH I COULD CHANGE THE PAST

I wish I could change the past,
So the cold dark nights would last.

I wish I could change the past,
So snails go fast.

I wish I could change the past,
So the weekend would last.

I wish I could change the past,
So I will go fast.

I wish I could change the past,
So the Baker day would last.

Kayleigh Gilfrin (10)
Lower Halstow Primary School

WHEN I GET TO SCHOOL I CAN HEAR . . .

When I get to school I can hear
children laughing and playing in
the playground.

When I get to school I can hear
teachers telling little children off
for talking in class.

When I get to school I can hear
people saying sorry I'm late again.

When I get to school I can hear
classes doing PE.

When I get to school I can hear
children crying because somebody
has pushed them over.

When I get to school I can hear
people playing It or Tag.

When I get to school I can hear
people shouting at each other.

When I get to school I can hear
people playing and climbing on
the climbing frame.

When I leave school
the day starts again.

Jaime Martin (11)
Lower Halstow Primary School

IN MY MAGIC TV SCREEN

In my magic TV screen
I see a dragon he looks mean.

In my magic TV screen
I see a flag that is bright green.

In my magic TV screen,
I see a golden jellybean.

In my magic TV screen,
I see an advert for a washing machine.

In my magic TV screen
Whahay it's Mr Bean.

Peter Clark (10)
Lower Halstow Primary School

I DID SOMETHING AND . . .

I shouted and shouted and
the walls came tumbling down.

I screamed and screamed and
it was even louder than a band.

I stomped and stomped and
I broke all the big windows in the house.

I banged and banged and
somebody opened the creaking door with a big furry hand.

I clapped and clapped and
every single person was at my service.

I shouted and shouted because
somebody tricked me it was all a dream!

Phillippa Calvert (9)
Lower Halstow Primary School

In My Strange Wardrobe

In my horrible wardrobe late at night I hear,
Creepy snakes slithering in and out with each other.

In my gloomy wardrobe late at night I hear,
Fluttering bats wildly tearing at my clothes.

In my dreadful wardrobe late at night I hear,
Tarantulas chewing my slippers and Nan's wig.

In my deafening wardrobe late at night I hear,
Helpless children screaming while bleeding to death.

In my ghastly wardrobe late at night I hear,
Skeletons rattling bones to sound out the night of spooks.

Krista Hogg (10)
Lower Halstow Primary School

I Ran Down The Stairs

I ran down my dreamful stairs,
And I saw myself playing for England.

I ran down my dreadful stairs,
And ugly snakes crawled up my arm.

I ran down my magic stairs,
And the whole world turned to white chocolate.

I ran down my disgusting stairs,
And I saw a dead disgusting mummy chasing me.

I ran down my caramel stairs,
And teachers turned to rich chocolate.

I ran down my Smartie stairs,
And Smarties turned to chocolate.

Reece Jacobs (10)
Lower Halstow Primary School

THE THIRTEENTH YEAR

In the thirteenth year
the wind blows like normal.

In the thirteenth month
glass windows smash.

In the thirteenth week
tall buildings sway.

In the thirteenth day
giant oak trees uproot
and land on people's houses.

In the thirteenth hour
massive skyscrapers collapse
and the worst hurricane begins.

In the thirteenth minute
everything is blown to smithereens.

In the thirteenth second
the whole universe blows up.

Bang! Aaahhhh.

Jemma Gardner (10)
Lower Halstow Primary School

AT MIDNIGHT

At midnight
I see plain people turn slowly inside out.

At midnight
I see little green aliens take over planet Earth.

At midnight
I see hungry giant moths eating tiny bats.

At midnight
I see gruesome people wake from the dead.

At midnight
I see horrible people turn to hungry vampires.

At midnight
I see giant swarms of mosquitoes.

At midnight
I see the whole wide world blow up forever.

Sara Watson (10)
Lower Halstow Primary School

WHEN I SNEEZE

When I sneeze,
Dusty books fall off the creaky shelves.

When I sneeze,
Windows shatter and smash into a million pieces.

When I sneeze,
Tall buildings fall down to the bumpy roads.

When I sneeze,
People die of insect bites and diseases.

When I sneeze,
Volcanoes explode and red hot, thick lava flows
Down the side of the gigantic volcanoes.

When I sneeze,
The world falls down, down, down . . .

Louise Smith (11)
Lower Halstow Primary School

IN MY HAUNTED HOUSE

In my haunted house
I hear black bats flapping their dirty wings noisily.

In my haunted house
I see blood-sucking vampires sucking blood from people's necks.

In my haunted house
I smell the witch's green brew burning in the old cauldron.

In my haunted house
I taste Dr Jeckyl's bright blue potion to become the dreadful
                                                    Mr Hyde.

In my haunted house
I dream I was a dead rotten mummy in dirty bandages.

In my haunted house
I sleep in a creaky bed with dusty bedcovers.

Daniel Bradford (10)
Lower Halstow Primary School

MY POEM

Ten little monkeys swinging on a line
One fell off
Then there were nine.

Nine little monkeys sitting on a gate
One fell down
Then there were eight.

Eight little monkeys looking up to heaven
One ran away
Then there were seven.

Seven little monkeys fetch some sticks
One got lost
Then there were six.

Six little monkeys went to a hive
One got stung
Then there were five.

Five little monkeys playing by the door
One got hurt
Then there were four.

Four little monkeys dropped their tea
One got burnt
Then there were three.

Three little monkeys went to the zoo
One got a lion
Then there were two.

Two little monkeys playing with a gun
One got shot
Then there was one.

One little monkey sucking his thumb
His mother called him in
Then there were none.

Katie Goss (10)
Northend Primary School

TEN LITTLE DEVILS

Ten little devils standing in a line
One got caught
Then there were nine

Nine little devils playing with a gate
One got squashed
Then there were eight

Eight little devils thinking about Devon
One went there
Then there were seven

Seven little devils playing with sticks
One got a splinter
Then there were six

Six little devils standing around a beehive
One got stung
Then there were five

Five little devils hanging round the door
One got locked in
Then there were four

Four little devils going for tea
One ate too much
Then there were three

Three little devils playing with glue
One got too sticky
Then there were two

Two little devils having some fun
One went home
Then there was one

One little devil sitting in the sun
He got burnt
Then there were none.

Billy Waterfall (9)
Northend Primary School

CATS

Ten little cats drinking wine
One got drunk
Then there were nine

Nine little cats swinging on a gate
One fell off
Then there were eight

Eight little cats going to heaven
One lost its wings
Then there were seven

Seven little cats playing with sticks
One poked his eye out
Then there were six

Six little cats having a dive
One got soaked
Then there were five

Five little cats who were poor
One fell over
Then there were four

Four little cats climbing a tree
One got stuck
Then there were three

Three little cats sitting in a queue
One got in the concert
Then there were two

Two little cats having fun
One had to go home
Then there was one

One little cat hurt his thumb
He had to go home
Then there were none.

Carly Maynard (9)
Northend Primary School

TEN LITTLE ANIMALS

Ten little animals saw people dine
One ate a person's dinner
Then there were nine

Nine little animals getting through a gate
One got stuck
Then there were eight

Eight little animals going to go to Devon
One did not get there
Then there were seven

Seven little animals going to get some sticks
One picked up a rose bush
Then there were six

Six little animals going to a hive
One got stung
Then there were five

Five little animals walking across the floor
One tripped up
Then there were four

Four little animals having some tea
One did not eat a lot
Then there were three

Three little animals went to the zoo
One got trapped in a cage
Then there were two

Two little animals went to have some fun
One got lost
Then there was one

One little animal thought he weighed a ton
He fell off the scales
Then there were none.

Karl Ansell (10)
Northend Primary School

TEN LITTLE BOYS

Ten little boys sneaking in line
One got caught
Then there were nine.

Nine little boys going to faint
One got blue
Then there were eight.

Eight little boys go to the same heaven
One turned into a devil
Then there were seven.

Seven little boys cooking and mixing
One got burned
Then there were six.

Six little boys had a big fight
One got punched
Then there were five.

Five little boys have their own part on the floor
One went off
Then there were four.

Four little boys sing in the tree
One fell off
Then there were three.

Three little boys singing in the zoo
One got sad
Then there were two.

Two little boys on the bus
One went to the town
Then there was one.

One little boy trying to have fun
One hurt his leg
Then there were none.

Eric (10)
Northend Primary School

THE BEAUTIFUL SIGHT

As I watched the sun go down
Emerging in and out of clouds
The spectrum of the sun glistened deep into
the calm sea water.
The warmth of the sky floated down onto my bare arms
I stood stone still staring at the crystals behind
the slowly breaking ripples.
That night was quiet
All that was to be heard was my slow breathing pattern
One day all of this would just be a memory.

Sarah Wreford (10)
Palm Bay CP School

MY SPEEDY SHARK

He is as fast as ten sports cars put together,
and as intelligent as Albert Einstein.
His biceps are as big as King Kong's!
He climbs the Empire State building every day
with Jupiter on his back.
He goes to Saturn for a trip and stops meteorites
from hitting the Earth.
He is the best mathematician in the solar system.
He is the greatest pet alive! (Well I think he is)

Oliver Harris (10)
Palm Bay CP School

PREDATOR

Running, running from any danger
The jungle terrors
make me weak
I collapse, the fear forcing me down
to the damp jungle floor
where predators roam
My heart pounding like a raging lion
waiting for the jaguar that seeks by blood
to pounce and end my petty life
Thoughts of pain bolted through my brain
every shadow, shaped as if spear-like claws
or fanged teeth
I got up and walked forward
too paralysed by fear to run
Suddenly my eyes shot to the side
and there my stalker stood
A shiver ran down my spine
I slowly moved away
his dark fleshy skin was red
from his last victim
A tear ran from my eye
as his evil glowing eyes stared at me
almost piercing through my skin
I walked backwards again then I fell
I could feel my head bang against a hard weed
then the jaguar pounced!

Adam Heather (10)
Palm Bay CP School

VENUS (THE ROMANTIC PLANET)

Venus is the planet of love
It has a lovely smell of perfume
Which makes all the other planets jealous
Colourful strips of unknown colours
Lovely shape made out of all different kinds
Of sweets like sherbet, lollies, Polos but not round,
Syrup, honey, *yummy.*
Slippery ice where the white bits show
But sometimes melt because there's no snow
The planet is hot like lava, it never rains
Because it's so hot it has not got a spot
like Jupiter.

For Venus is the planet of love.

Kelly Thorn (10)
Palm Bay CP School

THE SUN SETS

I gazed in awe out towards the sea
Watched it hungrily swallow up the shaded sun
The colours glistened, reflected across the subtle sky
I turned to watch the river
The bending river which fed the sea
Its waves gently rippled
As a nearby tree submerged one of its beautiful branches
Gently bathing it in the warm water.

Hollie Dixon (11)
Palm Bay CP School

THE FROSTY NIGHT

It's a very frosty night
My feet are cold
There I walked upon the icy road
Chattering teeth, freezing cold
How I wish I was in a nice warm home
The icy breeze swished around
How I wanted to scream
Aloud!

Sarah Pryor (11)
Palm Bay CP School

THE STORM

The lightning hits the darkened road
The thunder booms around the sky.
Raindrops falling down and down
Tapping on the windows then dropping to the ground.
These horrible storms make me quiver
The echoing noises make me shiver.

Emma Wallace (11)
Palm Bay CP School

RAINDRONE

Hot and sticky,
clear skies,
colourful ground,
flat and soft,
silent as nothing,
large leafy bushes like a giant cabbage,
glowing like shooting stars.

Stephanie Hackworth (10)
Palm Bay CP School

ALONE

You power up your booster rockets and try to escape
the black hole. But it pulls you in.
You emerge to find you're ten million years in the future.
You use your navigator computer to find Earth.
When you find Earth it has been destroyed only to find craters.
A great war had taken place with aliens.
You're alone - the last human ship in the universe.

Matthew Kelly (10)
Palm Bay CP School

MY IMAGINARY ELECTRIC BOX

My box is made of computer chips.
If anyone touches it they will get electrocuted.
My hinges are going to be made of 3500 volts.
The whole universe is going to be inside it.
I want it for when I go to bed.
I can look at it and I'm not scared
of the dark anymore.

Lee Huddleston (10)
Palm Bay CP School

MY IMAGINARY BOX

My lovely box is made of zebra skin
and my hinges are out of horse hair.
Inside my box will be a zoo
with zebras, monkeys, elephants and all
sorts of creatures.
The box is for making me feel happy
because I love animals.

Carlie Pearlman (10)
Palm Bay CP School

WAR 1939

1939 War is declared
1939 Homes are flared

1940 Sirens go off
1940 The smoke made me cough

1941 Bombs are dropped
1941 In the shelter I popped

1942 There's nothing I can do
1942 I left home too

1943 Get your gas mask out
1943 Don't walk about

1944 Bolt your door
1944 I can't take it anymore

1945 Peace is declared
1945 No longer scared.

Rebecca Huckstep (10)
Palm Bay CP School

EVACUATION

The thick smoke drifted
Up into the blackened atmosphere,
Caused by the creaking steam train
As if produced by a livid dragon.
The station master gave a huge blow
into his shining whistle.
As the train became mobile,
The children's mothers faded as
the train rolled along the rusty track.

Kieran Mannings (10)
Palm Bay CP School

DO YOU DARE GO DOWN NONSENSE STREET?

I was walking down the Nonsense Street backwards
and I saw
An organ grinder and his monkey knocking at the door.
Suddenly I saw with my left ear
a hipporhinocecow standing near,
Walking on, I spied its mate who had an even greater weight.
'Oh' I cried, 'Why don't you diet?'
and it bellowed, 'Oh do be quiet!'
As the organ went out of tune
the monkey floated off in a balloon.
I know not where it went, nor care
but the organ grinder complained to Tony Blair.

James Spear (9)
Palm Bay CP School

PLANET BONGZILIOUS

Meteors crashing, forcing great pressure onto Bongzilious.
A massive scorching hot blazing volcano in the centre
sends up thousands of litres of boiling hot lava:
Permanently frozen icy ground beneath the surface.
Boulders scattered everywhere.
You feel like there's death shrouds sneaking up behind you.
You can feel it, your instincts tell you.
The air is impossible to live upon.
For it's been sucked through maggot-infested sneakers,
thousands of years old.
The scenery is really freaky.
It reminds me of a massive black room.
You get lost for hours and hours.
You get very weary, gradually and slowly you die!

Johnathan Fell (10)
Palm Bay CP School

THE CAT

The cat slowly but cautiously slunk along the sturdy brick wall.
As it crept along my gaze followed it from the shiny window-pane
to the old forlorn shed.
Slowly the cat crawled through a broken window-pane,
Over some gardening pots.
I lost sight of it.
Then I heard a crashing and a tumbling.
It made my blood turn cold.
Then an angry barking and hissing and spitting.
All turned silent.
I knew the cat could not survive the
    red
       glaring eyes
            and
             gnashing
               sharp teeth.

Richard Gray (10)
Palm Bay CP School

SPIDER!

The splendid *spider!*
With hairy dangly legs as long as the M25.
His eyes are as big as 12 moons.
The shape of my spider is a hexagon.
The teeth are vampires' teeth.
It runs 5,000,000 miles per hour.
It's got muscles like an ant!
It eats terrifying teachers!
It drinks beetle juice.

Christopher Young (10)
Palm Bay CP School

SHADOWS IN THE NIGHT

I lie in bed staring up at my ceiling.
I hear the spooky church bells pealing.
I see shadows of bats, ghosts and scary faces.
Footsteps echoing on the landing as people take huge paces.
I can hear cats and dogs chasing each other up the road.
I can't get to sleep,
So I sit up and read the secret code.
I hear footsteps coming up the stairs 'Creak creak creak'
I hide down under my cover 'Deep deep deep.'
The lightshade makes a shadow on my ceiling
making a shape of a bat.
A shadow on my curtain in a shape of a cat.
Night is spooky night is bold night is scary when it's cold.
At last it's morning hooray hooray
Night-time's over hip hip hooray.

Tara Sutton (10)
Palm Bay CP School

STEAM TRAIN

Black smoke fills the air,
People scurry towards the train,
The train grinds to a halt.
I stare down at the dusty path,
A shiver runs down my small, cold spine,
I quickly open a creaky door,
Tapping sounds echo in my ears.
A whistle is blown, the doors slam,
Away!

Alice Martin (11)
Palm Bay CP School

MY SUPER-DUPER PET

My pet is a computer whiz, a great inventor too!
He thought of the Titanic and the flushing loo!
He eats only bacon, spaghetti and pork chops.
And eats even more when he gets gigantic spots.
He weighs more than an elephant and is bigger
than my house.
Inside he's like a kitten though, for he's scared of my mouse.
He makes a deep grunting noise when he gets upset,
this always happens when he loses on a bet.
He is the colour of deep blue and changes
from red to green too.
I never have to take him to the vet
for he's my *super-duper* pet!

Alexandra Pacey (9)
Palm Bay CP School

STARING

She's there all the time.
Staring
She looks at me all day.
Staring
Her eyes bloodshot with pain.
Staring
I look away but she's there.
Staring
Her eyes glaring at me.
Staring.

Amy Quy-Verlander (11)
Palm Bay CP School

THE OPPONENT

People walking down the street
Tired, lonely, dying of hunger
Needing assistance, needing help
People shaking, shattering, freaking out
Children stumble to the ground
As the colours of the rainbow
Glisten over the shining horizon
The floor starts to shake, the enemy
draws nearer, nearer
The open field draws closer, closer
Death is here
Blood overwhelms my body
Silence.

Alex Grace (10)
Palm Bay CP School

THE TORTOISE

He lifts his wrinkly legs,
And takes a sturdy stride,
For food he always begs,
He bows his head in pride,
Shuffling his legs through the sand,
Hiding from deadly predators,
The sun sets from the dark blue sky,
He slides back into his green mossed shell,
And falls into a deep, deep sleep.

Luke Dyer (11)
Palm Bay CP School

DEATH

Dark thoughts rush my mind
monotonously over and over
death death.
I sit in my rugged armchair
thinking about what may be if I go.
Suddenly, a sharp pain strikes me
in the heart, I'm dying.
My cup of coffee slips out of
my sweaty palms and smashes on
the shiny wood floor.
My wife walks in looking spellbound
at me dying.
She tries to save me but it's too late.

Phillip Alexandrakis (11)
Palm Bay CP School

MY SPECTACULAR BOX

My spectacular box is made from the weather.
The glimmering sun, the sparkling rain and the most
beautiful of rainbows.
The hinges are made from flower stems woven in and out.
When you open my box out will pop a huge beanstalk
which you will climb up in the air into the clouds
and your eyes will be amazed what fantasies there are.
Dragons soaring in the sky, sunflowers singing to the wind.
I would keep my box in my room to keep it safe
and secure.

Hannah Dunn (9)
Palm Bay CP School

SHIMMERING STARS

The lonely man looks up in the sky,
The shimmering stars catch his eye,
He wonders why they shine so bright,
And why they are there night after night,
The gloomy darkness fills his brain,
Maybe he is going insane,
He glares on into the night,
A twig brushed past him,
Giving him a fright,
He stares back into the stars,
He sees a planet,
Maybe it's Mars?
He turns away and goes back home,
Although the man is still on his own,
The shimmering stars make him smile,
Maybe he will only be on his own for a while.

Kirsty McChesney (11)
Palm Bay CP School

SUMMERTIME

Summertime is a beautiful thing,
The birds and the bees come out to sing.
Lambs and foals prance around,
When it's time to sleep they fall to the ground.
Red roses fill the garden with colour,
Weeds always make the garden seem duller.
When the sun shines brightly,
I feel like it's summertime.
My favourite part of the year.

Claire Tiley (10)
Palm Bay CP School

JUPITER

Jupiter's big red spot glows in the universe
as its bumpy moons twist around it.
Its colours are so bright
black, orange, red and white.
It stays still as the stars float by.
Jupiter is in the middle of Mars and Saturn
With a dark black background.

Jadie Hards (10)
Palm Bay CP School

JUPITER

Made of green slime with exploding rocks,
Making huge craters in the coloured chalk.
The heat of the sun makes the slime melt,
Dripping onto the planet Earth,
Polluting the air and the seas too.
The people on Earth don't know what to do,
Jupiter and Earth are slowly dying.
The heat of the sun is getting closer.

Charlotte Tournay (10)
Palm Bay CP School

THE MOST BEAUTIFUL BEACH IN THE WORLD

The stars twinkled in the sky
as I walked along the beautiful glistening sand.
I sat down and snuggled into the sand
thinking how lovely the beach was.
The peace and quiet was so nice
because I have noise all day.

Natalie Baughan (11)
Palm Bay CP School

LEAVING

I am leaving home
Not coming back.
I will have to reminisce
About the place called home
I am standing by myself
Staring hard
I don't want memories
I want to stay and live my life
Will I ever go back?
It's time to go away
It's time, time to be alone.

Philip Nesbit (11)
Palm Bay CP School

A SECRET

I was only ten as I walked down the road,
My mother was with me,
We passed the gate with patches of green,
Then we came across an old man who was
standing in a dark doorway,
'Good afternoon,' he said in a hoarse voice,
My mother stopped and talked to him,
I tugged my mother's arm I wanted to go,
The old man stared at me with his tired brown eyes,
Then he bent down,
His old dirty hands brought up a box,
The lid fell slowly off the box and onto the floor,
I looked in the box and something told me a secret.

Charlotte Ende (10)
Palm Bay CP School

MY LITTLE KITTEN

My little kitten runs about the house
upstairs and downstairs,
He's a little terror, he eats his food
then runs round like mad,
My little kitten runs about the house.

Emily Smith (9)
Parkwood Junior School

MY LITTLE PUPPY

My little puppy is as cute as can be
He has not got any fleas
He's black and white
and doesn't want to fight
My little puppy is as cute as can be.

Lucy Sibley-Hammond (9)
Parkwood Junior School

YOUNG LOVE

First you sing in the shower.
Then you get brain-washed with love.
Then you see him with your best friend.
Then you fight.
Then you win him back.
Young love isn't it sweet.

Elizabeth Hunt (9)
Parkwood Junior School

FRIENDSHIP

Sharing secrets
Meeting secretly
Baby-sitting
Sleepovers
Love-sick over boys
Just sick over pretty girls
They're always there to lighten the load
They're always there to make it heavier
Friendship is like a jigsaw
Lose a piece, everything's lost
Pulled apart, everything's a mess
Glued together, everything's perfect
What crazy ups and downs friendship's got
But I'd go through them a thousand times just
To see the smile at the end.

Ramandeep Goraya (11)
Rosherville CEP School

A QUIET DAY

One day it was *so* quiet
I could hear
The rainbow's colours shining
A mouse walking on the snow
Birds flying through the sky
A boy reading a book
The wind blowing
The leaves from a tree
And falling onto the ground
It was *so* quiet.

Sunpreet Burrha (8)
Rosherville CEP School

A Quiet Day

One day it was *so* quiet
I could hear
The flowers growing slowly,
The beautiful leaves falling
Quietly onto the ground,
The beautiful rainbow coming
into the sky,
The colourful balloons floating gently upwards,
The fishes swimming peacefully in the sea,
The beautiful sunset over the sea,
The bright sun stretching in the sky,
The worms swirling on the ground calmly.
It was so quiet.

Gurpreet Lalli (9)
Rosherville CEP School

The Quiet Day

One day it was *so* quiet
I could hear,
Rainbow colour appearing,
Lobsters dancing,
The balloon gently flying to heaven,
Rivers flowing,
The Earth moving round the sun,
Stars shining in the night,
Ribbons flying in the sky,
It was *so* quiet.

Devinder Singh (8)
Rosherville CEP School

MY SISTER

My sister is burnt black
She is a snake
My sister is a tornado
She is a pair of tatty old gloves
My sister is an antique
She is the next Cilla Black
My sister is a plate of burnt Brussel sprouts
That's my sister!

Sukhjit Klair (11)
Rosherville CEP School

IT WAS SO QUIET

One day it was *so* quiet
I could hear
Lee thinking lovely thoughts
Whales singing in the sea
Monkeys swinging in the jungle
Trees whispering to each other
Romans marching
Butterflies singing
It was so quiet.

Arjun Tehara (8)
Rosherville CEP School

QUIET DAY

One day it was so quiet
I could hear the flowers growing
in summer
The leaves falling to the ground
India singing in the summer for
Lohri Celebration
Balloons floating to heaven
It was so quiet.

Mahanvir (8)
Rosherville CEP School

IT WAS SO QUIET

One day it was so quiet
I could hear
The fishes breathing in the pond
A peaceful sunset in the sky
The tree swirling side to side
Angels dancing in heaven
And the children soundly asleep -
In their beds
It was so quiet.

Amanda Jane Rose Victoria Horrobin (8)
Rosherville CEP School

QUIET DAY

One day it was *so* quiet,
I could hear ballerinas
Softly dancing;
Spring in the wind
Blowing the clouds;
A shooting star flying
across the sky;
And flowers growing.
It was so quiet.

Spencer Roberts (8)
Rosherville CEP School

THE QUIET DAY

One day it was *so* quiet
I could hear
Balloons beautifully floating
into the air
Children working hard
Ribbons floating softly into the sky
The gold rays from the beautiful sun
The Earth spinning around the sun
It was *so* quiet.

Joanna Taylor (8)
Rosherville CEP School

My World

There are good things in the world,
But they are destroyed by pollution litter and drugs
Animals are killed each day
People are murdered or kidnapped by sick-minded people.

My ideal world would be filled with animals and trees,
But trees are cut down,
Countries are bombed each day,
What a sad world it is.

Could we change our world if we tried really hard?
Could we stop pollution and murders?
Could we stop trees being cut down and destroyed?
Oh what a lovely world it could be!

Jamie Shipp (10)
St Mary's CE Primary School, Swanley

My World

My world what a wonderful place to be,
Animals everywhere running free,
But my world would not be a world without
My friends and family,
The only thing is all the bad things,
Things like drugs and pollution.

My world what a wonderful place to be,
Rainbows flashing all around me,
But my world would not be a world without,
All the sports and games I play.

Sarah Maxey (10)
St Mary's CE Primary School, Swanley

MY WORLD

See animals playing
And people saying ahh!
Rainbows in the sky,
Fluffy clouds go by.
This world can be bad
Because of drugs and cigars.
People die of them and that is sad,
Animals can be fun.
People play in the warmth of the sun.
I like my world because of friends and family.
Wine and beer can make you drunk
Sniffing things you shouldn't do can kill you.
People don't really care about the world.
But I do.

Mary-Anne Hole (10)
St Mary's CE Primary School, Swanley

MY WORLD

My world is a wonderful place to be,
For people, creatures and also for me.
There are places in our world like:
The vets,
For our pets.

Pollution destroys
For women, men, girls and boys.
Bad things let our world down,
But let's not give up!
Let's keep going,
For the sake of my poem!

Debbie Blount (10)
St Mary's CE Primary School, Swanley

My World

In my world we watch the creatures walk and crawl,
I love my work that I do in school.
What would I do without the TV,
And my friends and family.
But things can ruin my world like:
Pollution and oil in the sea,
And it spoils the health of you and me.
People take things and all kinds of drugs,
People are bullied by all kinds of thugs.
Now I hope my poem has set you straight,
Stay with your friends and all your mates.

Natasha Taylor (10)
St Mary's CE Primary School, Swanley

My World

My world is full of flowers as well as enemy powers,
It is a wonderful place but people are ill or kill.
Strangely there are nuns with guns,
People make this place dirty, sometimes people die at thirty.
Maybe we could make this world better,
If we tried a little harder.
All the things that I like could be spoiled by a fight,
So if you live to ninety, read my poem every night.

Trevor Aslan (9)
St Mary's CE Primary School, Swanley

My World

My world is a lovely world
With the warm sun and the rain
The flowers, birds and creatures
But there are people ill who cry in pain.

The pollution spoils my world each day
And people shout and have their say
We could stop pollution
If we had a solution.

Hailey Cook (10)
St Mary's CE Primary School, Swanley

MY WORLD

There's a rumbling tumbling noise coming from those trees,
The trees are swaying in the breeze,
Or are they?

Smoke is filling the air
With gases I can't bear.

Hedgehogs are running,
Birds are humming.

Tractors churning,
Trees burning.
Oh what a sad world this is.
Or is it?

Foxes might be crying,
Animals might be dying.

But for each tree that is dug up
One is planted.

Daffodils, pansies, roses and tulips,
The biggest wish that can be granted.

Is our world free from destruction?

Bradley Smith (11)
St Mary's CE Primary School, Swanley

My World

Seeing baby animals in the fields.
Birds singing in the trees.
The warm sun shining on the plants.
I like the buzzing bees.
This world is a great place to live.

Things ruin my world like drugs and pollution.
My ideal world would be full of animals,
But I would not know what to do without my computer,
And my friends and family.
This world would be great without the bad things
                              that spoil it.

Christina Matthews (11)
St Mary's CE Primary School, Swanley

My World

There are beautiful things in this world
Like baby animals, but most are killed.
The warmth of the sun,
And the pictures that the snow makes,
And the beautiful rainbows in the sky.

I like playing netball with friends and family,
Playing on my computer and watching TV
On Saturdays my dad sits and watches
                              football all day long.

The best thing about this world is having
                    friends and a happy family,
But there are things that spoil our world
Like *drugs* and *litter.*

Tanya Jarrett (11)
St Mary's CE Primary School, Swanley

THE CANDLE

I am a candle,
tall and bright.
With a wick in the middle,
to give out light.

I come in all colours and lengths,
a symbol of love, light and strength.

I am found in churches,
homes and places.
Light me up and see
bright faces.

At birthday parties children shout,
'Happy birthday!' and blow me out.
On the mantle on my brass holder
Christmas gone,
another year older.

Now it's winter I will do my best,
and summertime I will take a rest.
I told my story,
now it's done.
Blow me out,
'God Bless Everyone!'

Teagan Trinkwon (12)
Sittingbourne Community College

THE CANDLE POEM

I am a candle
Straight and tall
I am a good candle most of all
Mostly I'm sad
I have no feet
But I am very neat
My flame alone can only move
It's wavy, it has a blazing light
I shrink minute by minute
My spirit is fading
I'm proud I'm happy
I'm getting very light
I'm an emotional candle
Now I'm fading to the ground
Next to no feet.

Nicola Palfreyman (9)
Thames View Junior School

THE DEAD CANDLE

One night I saw a candle swaying all alone
bashful, shy, looking claustrophobic in a scanty little jar.
I can hear it crying to itself, sobbing, sniffing, muttering.
I'm so small and lonely, blow me out, I'm not evil,
I want to live and I'm not bad.
As I thought he just shrivelled up and died.
But I'm sad because his spirit is free
and floating up in the lonely sky.
I'm cross with myself because I should have blown
the suffering candle out.
But I'm happy in a way because he is free and so am I.

Donna Cullen (9)
Thames View Junior School

THE FLAME'S BODY

An inside body
A peculiar flame
Emotional and scared
Shy, embarrassed, full of shame.

An evil flickering of light
Sometimes sad
Blazing, flicking bright
Sometimes bad.

A superb flame
Fading, fading
Into thin air
And deciding where to go
Forever lost
No return.

A dancing king
Coat upon coat
Of wax
'Hi!
My name is Max.

I'm a sad flame
I get embarrassed
I've got to flee
From this cold, dark room.'

Fiona Tullett (10)
Thames View Junior School

101 DALMATIANS

Pongo and Perdi met in the park,
All day long they had a good lark.
They loved it when they fell in the pond,
Soon they formed a loving bond.

Roger and Anita finally married,
And Roger the husband gratefully carried,
His wife Anita to the car,
What a great family they really are!

Cruella De Vil took the puppies away,
Pongo and Perdi wait day after day.
The Dalmatian dogs couldn't wait any more,
Pongo and Perdi ran out of the door.

The two poor dogs had run a mile,
When they got there, they waited a while.
Finally the little puppies came through,
Especially the little fat one too!

Pongo and Perdi had an excited yap,
The tiny puppies had a little nap.
The dogs were happy they were home,
Tired little puppies with their toy gnomes.

Stephanie Gilbert (10)
Thames View Junior School

FLICKING, TALL CANDLE

The flicking, flowing, sparkling, proud candle.
It glows all night, it is proud of itself.
It is a bright spirit, a tall shy candle.
The crystal clear light rushed past.

The sad little candle
Through the night room
No friends or comfort around
He flickers and dies.

Stacey William (9)
Thames View Junior School

THE HARE AND THE TORTOISE

Hare challenged Tortie to a race,
Tortie had horror on his face,
Hare came quickly, stood up straight,
He made it on time but Tortie was late.

The hare thought he would be first,
Unless the finish line was cursed,
Tortie knew he would be last,
He knew the hare was just too fast.

The race's course goes through the tip,
Hare was sleepy, so he had some kip,
Tortie was standing on the starting line,
Hare knew Tortie wouldn't make it on time.

Hare awoke and took a glance,
And saw Tortie way in the distance,
Hare got up and started to run,
Tortie was winning, he thought this was fun.

Hare started running, as fast as he could,
Hare must win, of course he would.
Hare ran quickly, just in time,
To see Tortie walk past the finish line.

Karen Parish (11)
Thames View Junior School

FLICKERING FLAMMABLE FLAME

At the start the flame's low,
Then the flame starts to glow,
As you gaze,
The light will blaze,
The night is dark,
The light will spark.

The wax melts
As I knelt
But the flame
Which magically came
With a little help from a match
The wax will melt
Because it's hot
The flame's near
But don't give fear
Then I smelled smoke,
I woke
I had to get to a smoke alarm
But it's a candle
So I can stay calm
Ring the fire bell
I will tell
The flame got bigger
Blow it out
Phew . . . now it's safe
But now it's dark.

Matthew Mole (9)
Thames View Junior School

Moving From Memories

Waking up and seeing the boxes,
Feeling confused and lost,
Coming downstairs and seeing,
Seeing, the living room,
Bare and uncosy, the high fire gone,
The couch, the TV all gone,
The memories of this room,
All my parties,
It feels like a draught has blown through,
My dog seems lost for her basket,
The kitchen, no food, no drink,
All the great food of this room,
Gone, never to taste right again,
Mum and Dad's room,
The bed I used to jump on,
Seeing my teddy bear, being taken downstairs,
'No, he comes with me!'
A big blue van pulls up,
Two strange men jump out,
They take the belongings of this home,
Putting them in the van,
'Please be careful,'
Soon the time comes,
The time to take my last step and my last look,
I cannot look back at the memories,
I cannot change the past,
Of my years in my home.

Daniel Dowsing (10)
Thames View Junior School

CANDLE

The candle with its brilliant light,
And dazzling flame brightens up the night.
Then as it brightens up the dark,
Out of it comes tiny sparks.

As I look down the hall,
It casts great shadows on the wall.
When the flame did appear,
It filled my body full of fear.

As I watched the golden glow,
The light seemed to have things to show.
It seemed that with its wonderful gleam,
That I was in a magical dream.

When the candle's bright light came,
I watched its red and golden flame.
A wonderful feeling I felt,
When the wax started to melt.

Dancing shadows upon the wall,
Where once there were none at all!

Hannah Baker (9)
Thames View Junior School

THE CANDLE

The candle is huge and proud
But as soon as it is lit the candle will fade down
The flame is wavy, spiteful, it is quite tall
But now it is fading, it is getting quite small
Now it's dying and in seconds it is gone
But its spirit will live on.

Daniel Sperrin (9)
Thames View Junior School

THREE LITTLE PIGS

The three little pigs went out one day
Building their houses in which to play.
The first one built his house of straw
And then it came crashing to the floor.

The second one built his house of sticks
The third one built his house of bricks
The big bad wolf along he came
He was not nice, he was not tame.

The wolf blew down the house of sticks
The pig ran to the house of bricks
The wolf climbed up the chimney top
And fell into the cooking pot.

Samantha Hewish (11)
Thames View Junior School

THE MOST ASTONISHING CANDLE

One night I saw a candle,
It had a miniature handle,
It was so small,
While I was so tall,
That I could hardly see it.
It thought it was in trouble,
I blew a tiny bubble,
It stood still and calm,
I put it on my palm,
It was glimmering,
I stood shimmering,
But of course,
It is a candle,
With a miniature handle.

Steven Smith (10)
Thames View Junior School

FLAME

I feel proud,
Dancing, twisting, quivering, flickering.

I feel elegant,
Blazing, revealing a red and orange
Spark to my flame.

I feel sad,
My spirit is fading, dying, shrinking,
Just like the others.

I feel vicious, ferocious,
I catch you in my spell.

I feel sizzling, glowing,
Making ripples in my skin
The ripples getting bigger
And I'm getting smaller.

Katie Hebditch (9)
Thames View Junior School

MONKEYS

Furry, brown creatures,
Hanging from trees,
Tails swinging, feet running,
Climbing with ease.

Devouring many bananas,
All day, every day,
Clutching them in soft paws,
Throwing the skins away.

Screeching and shouting,
Calling to anyone,
High-pitched shrieks,
Annoying everyone.

But, anyway,
I think they're funny,
The adorable, sweet,
Little monkey.

Laura Ray (10)
Thames View Junior School

SEASONS (HAIKU)

Autumn
The immense trees die
I trudge on the crisp, brown leaves
Temperatures fall.

Winter
Gusts of frosty wind,
Frozen ponds are hazardous
Polished snow falls down.

Spring
The air turns tepid
Animals give birth to young
Sparrows return home.

Summer
Beautiful mornings
Adolescent animals
Fruit is ripening.

Ben Manuel (11)
Thames View Junior School

THE FLICKERING CANDLE

On a stormy night,
The lights go out,
You have to put up the flickering candle.

The one certain candle,
The one candle that gives light,
With the hot burning candle,
You can see the tears go down
Its waxy body.

Its head is burning,
You can hear its cry from the fire,
It cries for help,
Its tears grow bigger and bigger.

The shiny flame flickering in the night,
The smoke grows thicker and thicker.
On a stormy night,
The candle goes out,
And the lights go on.

Amy Warner (9)
Thames View Junior School

FLAME

I feel like dancing beautifully
Twisting up and down
I am proud to be a glowing, flickering candle
I will be a crystal clear, glowing, sparkling candle
Going to and fro
My flickering body is blazing in the cold.

Natasha Risely (9)
Thames View Junior School

Sunny Day At The Beach

The sun is shining in the sky,
We are going to the beach,
Hip hip hooray
Get the spades and buckets ready,

Pile onto the train, doors slam shut
Gazing out of the window as the train whizzes
Past.
Pile off the train and run towards the beach,
Children scream I can see the sea.

Run towards the deep blue sea
Children screaming for an ice-cream,
Swimming in the sea
Waves come splashing at us.

Time to go home back to the train
Children fall asleep on the train,
Off at the station
Go all the way home.

Megan Kelly (8)
Thames View Junior School

Candle

C andle flickering fierce, hot
A larm when smoke hits the ceiling
N othing can stop the melting slippery wax
D estroying everything in its path
L ighting up the room with its hot light
E ntering the room with its hot glow.

Ryan Joy (10)
Thames View Junior School

THE DANCING CANDLE

The flame is flickering
fast and firm
With mighty strength
the wick it burns.

The dancing flame shimmers
up and down
Sometimes it might even
spin around.

The beautiful colours
let out a sparkling light
If you look at it close
it makes a beautiful sight.

George Broom (10)
Thames View Junior School

THE COUNTRYSIDE

Flowers are growing
Trees are blowing
Boats are rowing
Rivers are flowing
Sheep are baaing
Cows are mooing
Children are playing
People are praying
These are the sounds of the countryside.

Faye Andrew (9)
Thames View Junior School

THE CANDLE

The candle's flame flickering here and there
Watery wax dripping down the candle
The hot wax dripping down down down
The flame glowing bright and fierce
The smoke from the flame sets off the smoke alarm
People sit around it as they eat their tea.

The candle flickers so bright
The smell of smoke in the air
Bright colours, yellow, red and orange
The candle getting smaller and smaller
The room is getting darker and darker
As the candle dies out.

Katie Dearden (9)
Thames View Junior School

MOVING

I never wanted to move,
There was nothing I could do,
I felt helpless, lonely,
A stranger,
In a room that belonged to me.
Boxes piled up in dusty corners,
Out of the way for the moment,
Packed with all the accessories,
That made my home special.
Moving away from everything,
That I knew,
Felt I was being,
Forced from a place that,
I belonged to.

Stephanie Coombes (11)
Thames View Junior School

THE CANDLE

The candle flickers in the night.
As the candle's flame
Tries to light the dark gloomy room
It tries to frighten the darkness out of sight.

The candle's wax drips down the side.
The wax, damp, moist and watery.
The wax is like a falling tide.

As the candle goes away,
The wax has a last meltdown,
But the smell lives on.

Kirsty Logan (9)
Thames View Junior School

CANDLE

My candle flickers in the night,
Smelly, colourful and bright.

My little candle's very hot,
Making my brother glow in his cot.

His little flame is his hat,
Red enough to frighten the cat.

Blue, red, black and green,
My little candle's flame is mean.

My little candle is going down,
And I am starting to frown.

Poor little candle now has gone,
My little candle shone.

Amy Spray (9)
Thames View Junior School

CANDLE

The night came,
It woke up the flame.
It lit up the hall,
You could see it on the wall.
It was prancing,
And dancing,
It would gleam,
And you could just stand there and dream.

You could go near and,
It would appear,
That the bigger the glow,
The more it will show.
If you frown,
The light may go down,
And may never ever come back.

Cara Nicholson (10)
Thames View Junior School

THE CANDLE

The flickering light of the candle so bright
The candle so hot so embarrassed so shocked
The melting was so bright and hot
The candle of light the candle so bright
The candle of fame flickering so bright so light
Fear of the children as they watch the shocked candle
People come to see my little candle
People come for the bright flickering flame
Little candle so bright but so quiet.

Stephanie Chaplin (9)
Thames View Junior School

CANDLE

The flickering flame of my candle
flickers in the dark
The colours are
gold, yellow, amber, orange and red
As I watch the candle burn
The hot wax trickles down the side.

When my candle is around
he lights the darkness all around
Don't go too close to my candle
or he'll burn you
I sometimes see the smoke as it floats
into the sky
but my candle doesn't last forever
the wax soon will be gone.

Laura Dampier (9)
Thames View Junior School

THE CANDLE OF LIFE

The candle of life has power and
fame,
The candle of life has a yellow
flame.
The candle of life has wax and
joy,
The babies laugh at it with great
joy,

But then the wax melts away,
and there's nothing left for the
babies to play.

Paul Saunders (10)
Thames View Junior School

BURNING WAX

Why does a candle look so sad?
Shimmering, crackling day and night,
Waxy teardrops fall so slow,
A burning head,
Thinking what to do.

Why is the candle such a funny shape?
Twisting, shaking to and fro,
Worrying teardrops, falling deep,
A melting body,
Full of woe.

But the candle will not hide,
The candle with a timid character,
Shows its light and power,
Mighty thoughts and dreams,
Blowing down.

Lucy Woolford (10)
Thames View Junior School

LOVE

I love them so,
They are my heart,
I love them more than anybody and anything,
They give me things they should not do,
They give me more presents than I ask for,
They give me a happy life all the years through,
I love them with all my heart,
They mean the world to me,
Because they are my parents.

Jessica Read (9)
Thames View Junior School

OH NO! MONDAY!

I dread going to school on a Monday,
Not knowing who it will be next,
All my friends run to the hopscotch,
Whilst I just walk and stare,
Ready to be ambushed.

They're so clever,
They do it,
So no one knows,
But,
When Friday comes,
I have to look forward,
To someone else,
Next week!

Natasha Tiwari (9)
Thames View Junior School

IN THE WOODS

In the woods the birds sing,
In the wind the trees blow,
In the woods the leaves scatter,
Away in the woods they go.

The leaves in autumn go along,
They scatter all the way,
The leaves fall off,
And now they are all gone.

Now it is November,
I wish it was December,
Going all the way,
Goodbye!

Shelley Tapsell (11)
Thames View Junior School

THE BULLY

I was standing near the wall,
A boy coming towards me,
Thinking he was coming
To beat me up.
The next minute,
He pushed me,
Towards the wall,
I screamed.
There were more bullies coming,
I called the teacher,
She saw,
Then the bullies got expelled,
No more bullies
Around me now.

Lucy Rees (10)
Thames View Junior School

MY FRIEND, THE VICTIM

I stood behind the wall
disgusted that my friend
actually went
        to be bullied.

The bully always waits
at the back of the shed
I can't believe she goes just
        to be bullied.

She gives them her dinner money
and maybe her tuck,
she is bribed to do this
        her bad luck.

Atina Ellis (10)
Thames View Junior School

MOVING HOUSE

Memorable moments were left behind,
Seeing boxes being piled into the van,
Seeing the minutes go by,
Saying goodbye to my childhood house,
Saying goodbye to the moment I lost,
Seeing the faces of my helpless family,
Seeing the only house I ever knew, float into the distance,
Feeling my stomach churn.
Feeling as though I had nothing left,
Feeling like a mouse in a huge empty place,
As the boxes come into an old creaky hallway,
Isolated, confused and uneasy was how I felt,
Like a helpless, young stranger with no one to care.
An empty feeling, with an icy cold heart,
As a small, lonely figure stepped into a dark room,
As I settled into a new, fresh home,
A home that was there to protect me,
From the cold icy winds and those long, spooky nights,
A home that was there to protect me,
My home.

Natalie Jane Read (11)
Thames View Junior School

MY RABBIT

My rabbit's name is Thumper
He jumps about all day
Eating Mummy's flowers
And chasing birds away.

My rabbit's name is Thumper
He's soft and furry to touch
I give him lots of food and hay
When he's in his hutch.

My rabbit's name is Thumper
He's white and black and grey
He loves it when I brush him
Nearly every day.

My rabbit's name is Thumper
He lives in a great big hutch
I go to see him every day
Because I love him very much.

Kimberley Platt (9)
Thames View Junior School

THE DYING FLAME

The blazing, shimmering spirit,
Is fading away,
The flame is packing,
Away his only gift.
His only proud friend,
He's sadly, shrinking down,
Into his gloomy cave,
His crystal clear spirit,
Will rise again,
One bright, blazing day.
Sadly the shimmering flame,
Dies down thinking.
Shrinking is going to happen,
I'm not proud.
I'm sore again.

Laura Ellis (10)
Thames View Junior School

CANDLE

The candle is so very hot,
that smoke is coming out a lot!
It is getting shorter and shorter,
dripping wax like running water.
As it burns people start to gaze,
looking at its fiery blaze.

I imagine how the candle felt,
when all the wax started to melt.
It is so light and so very bright,
it can light up the whole of the night.
Also used for decorations,
and even for big celebrations.

The candle has a very bright gleam,
and also a very big beam.
Touch the flame if you dare,
candles can be anywhere!
In the hall,
by the wall,
in a church,
where shadows lurk,
in an old room,
that brightens up the gloom,
in a castle it will glare,
candles can be anywhere!

Jonathan Costello (10)
Thames View Junior School

ICE SKATING

I think there's nothing as nice
As skating on my own ice
When I go skating up and down
My voice is the dearest wonderful sound.

My clothes shimmer and look
As an adventure book
When I grow up I will skate under the frosty moonlight
So in the morning I'll just say I want to stay all day.

Amanda Holmes (11)
Thames View Junior School

THE DISASTER STRUCK ENVIRONMENT

Trees very dead,
Plants lying flat down,
Animals coughing,
Including us, too!

More and more,
Pollution is coming from us,
Cars, power stations,
More every day.

The world would be nice,
Without the rubbish,
No crisp packets choking plants, or
Plastic bags hanging on the trees.

We could have heaven,
Instead we have hell,
We can save our land,
Without the pollution.

Without the pollution,
It would be clean,
Without the pollution,
The environment is kind to
Us and animals.

Michael Rose (11)
Thames View Junior School

THE MAGIC OF THE NIGHT

As the blazing light,
Fills the dark night sky,

The flame shimmers,
Jolts as the wind softly blows.

As the shady moonlight beams,
The spirited candle is proud to help it,
Gleaming through the thick night clouds.

The dazzling flames are dancing freely,
To the sweet music of the whisking wind.

While the nocturnal animals are creeping,
They have the tender candle to lead the way.

All of this is but so beautiful,
And as the red hot sun rises softly,

The crystal flame dies out,
Melts away, fading silently without a trace.

It's gone
I can still feel the dreamy spirit,
Floating softly around me
I feel dazed, as light as a feather,

And now I say farewell,
To a dream I'll never forget.

Lauren Mason (10)
Thames View Junior School

AUTUMN PARK

Brown, red and golden leaves,
Tumble in the frozen breeze,
Rain is falling in the park,
Reminds me of Noah in the ark.

Screaming winds weave in and out,
And the mighty trees are about to shout,
Look out here comes the frost,
Giving the air a nasty bite,
November the plants are in such a fright,
I hope the birds have flown away,
Far from the weather we've had today.

Laura Knight (10)
Thames View Junior School

THE FLAME'S LIFE STORY

The wick
Sits
In its dead waxy coat
Then life!
Gets hotter in the white jacket
The mystical light grows,
A poisonous smoke,
Raises,
With a burnt, misty aroma.

The spirit gets higher, higher,
Hovering over the soapy mass
Of soggy wax
Puff!
A breeze sucks out the life
All that is left,
Is the lumpy, dry, cold wax
The long, black dehydrated wick
The lingering aroma,
Burnt,
Dead.

Stevie-Louise Attwood (10)
Thames View Junior School

THE MAGIC CANDLE

The candle is lit clear and bright,
As the proud candle melts to the ground,
The over-reacting evil candle is melting with a happy cry,
The flickering shimmering candle is crying happily,
As it waves here and there,
The candle is getting too embarrassed,
So blow out the candle as it dies,
Then let the candle glow again,
For once and for all.

Katrina Gordon (10)
Thames View Junior School

VOLCANO ESCAPADE

A volcano's erupting, got to bike,
Must take five things I quite like.

I think my family I should take,
Just in case there is a quake.

I think I'll take my crocodile,
Because he can run the minute mile.

I'll take his friend the grey Chihuahua,
Because he can run on red hot lava.

I'll take my car, a red Mercedes,
Because it impresses all the ladies.

I'll take some shoes, some things to wear,
Just in case the weather' fair.

At last we've settled in a home,
In a special volcano free dome.

Jamie Rayner (11)
Thames View Junior School

CANDLE

The flame is sizzling,
wavy,
The flame is dancing
side to side
Up and down, smooth and
soft,
With the wax dripping
down the candle.
Getting smaller and
smaller.
It's gleaming, glistening,
glowing and shimmering
Sparkling and shining
it is bold and fierce
Fiery and timid
strong and flickering.

Lee Grainger (10)
Thames View Junior School

MY DOG BENJI

He knows when I am upset and lonely
He knows I care for him
I would do anything for him because he
Is precious to me.
If he is hurt I look after him
He trusts me all the time.
We have lots of fun together
And he will always be my friend
      Benji.

Katie Hawes (10)
Thames View Junior School

MOVING OUT

We're moving away to where the bird sings,
I'll take with me five of my things,
The first thing has got to be my mum,
She's more special to me than anyone,
Second has to be my mum's boyfriend, Mark,
Whose skin is soft and hair is dark.
Third is Zoë, my little sister,
'Cause if I'd left her I'd only have missed her,
And of course I'd take Flopsy,
My rabbit just has to come with me,
My teddies wouldn't miss out on coming,
Because who would play with them and take them running,
So away we have to go,
Driving over roads, high and low.

Sian Harvey (11)
Thames View Junior School

THE CANDLE

A child stared at the flickering candle
The child blew out the light.
From the candle
Embarrassed colours
Yellow, red and pink with smoke
Watery and dripping liquid from the wax
Fierce with scare and heat.
People looking at the embarrassed candle
With red faces
Flickering in fear
Melting with wax
Dripping down the side.

Natasha Blundell (10)
Thames View Junior School

THE CANDLE

The flame is flickering side to side
It's a sudden bright burst of a light
A device for making a brief bright light
By which to take photographs.

The flame is like the sun and moon
Flickering side to side like illumination.
Immediately a bright burst of light
To appear suddenly.

To move quickly like a train
Flashed past like a bright light.
The brilliance, glowing illumination
Of radiation.
I am a flame.

Wesley Larkin (9)
Thames View Junior School

CANDLE POEM

The proud twisting spirit
Its fearless blazing light
The bashful, embarrassed flame

Its shy flickering spirit
Its troubled shimmering flame
The shallow candle

Ready to comfort you
Its strong blazing flame
Its shrinking fading light
Its ever flickering flame.

Craig Oldershaw (9)
Thames View Junior School

BEST FRIENDS

Playing with each other every day,
Doing things together in a special way,
At lunch-time sharing food,
Both of us being good,
Working together,
Best friends forever,
Each other opening the door,
That's what friends are for.

Lisa Hills (10)
Thames View Junior School

UNCARING WORLD

Today is a reality,
Countryside, trees and beautiful
Fields of corn,
Tomorrow a vision of dust,
Factories and despair,
In a world with no love,
A world that doesn't
Care . . .

Stacie Eriksson (11)
Thames View Junior School

ENVIRONMENT

Pollution is a predator,
Stalking, killing all around,
Green, brown, clear bottles recycle
Animals are dying, help!

Do your part to help recycle
Don't discard your man-made waste,
Pick up litter in the street,
Plastic recycling bins.

Amy Bourne (10)
Thames View Junior School

LAND OF LAVA

This land is made of lava,
It turns harder and harder and harder,
It has no sun, no moon, no fun, it's just a
Massive planet.

This land has lots of mountains,
It also has some fountains,
They're big, red, come above your head,
On the land of lava.

The sky is as black as night,
The day has no light,
The rocks below are as white as snow,
Fatal when you fall.

When you visit this place,
You'll have a look on your face,
There's nothing to see, nothing to do
Apart from the red hot goo.

There is nothing else to say,
So I'll be on my way,
I'll get back home by using the phone,
Catch the interspace express.

Chella Williams (11)
Thames View Junior School

THE CANDLE POEM

I am the candle
That stands on the mantlepiece,

Tall and straight,
With the gleaming flame,
Orange and brown,
I warn people to not touch me.

I'm warm and hot,
So you shouldn't touch me,
Because I'll burn you.

My wick melts,
When the flame
Is burning,
So don't touch me!

Michelle Healey (9)
Thames View Junior School

CANDLE FLAME

The big, proud, evil,
Shimmering light waving shyly
Goodbye.
The flickering, sad light,
Shrinking away.
The bad, fearless, blazing
Flame.
The flame hiding in its
Shy dark corner.
Shrinking away softly and
Crying for the last time.

Christopher McGarry (10)
Thames View Junior School

THE SEASONS

Acorns on the ground,
Colourful leaves on the floor,
People sweep them up.

People wrap up warm,
Children's toes are very cold,
Snowballs thrown for fun.

Sunshine warms the earth,
Birds are singing in the trees,
Daffodils are nice.

It is very hot,
Families go to the beach,
Strawberries and cream.

Can you guess which season is which?

Katherine Wisdom (10)
Thames View Junior School

THE SPARKLY CANDLE

Sizzling, sparkly, spluttering candle
Baking, stormy flames
Proud, embarrassed and sad.

Curly, dazzling, stunning candle
Some tall, some small, extremely tiny
Some are going to melt up and die.

Steaming, fierce looking candle
Shimmering, flickering, brilliantly
Sweltering in the bright bronze pot.

Charlotte Louise Comer (9)
Thames View Junior School

MY SPECIAL FRIEND

She is always close to me,
I could not live without her,
She always senses my feelings,
She knows my thoughts,
She is really loving,
I feel safe with her,
She is really precious to me,
She is priceless.

Who is it?

It is you, Mum.

Hannah Jordan (10)
Thames View Junior School

PROJECTS

At school I love projects, I always do 'birds',
I quite like the drawing, just can't do the words.
Try as I might the ideas won't come,
I'm ever so glad when it's time to go home.

I do like the projects I find them quite fun,
But I long for the day I shout 'It's all done!'
Put down my pen as the light starts to go,
I felt really shattered, carried on although,

I find it frustrating, when I work each night,
I copy out notes, then have to rewrite,
I thought I might cheat and copy a verse,
But after an hour it made matters worse.

I did this at breakfast in a terrible hurry,
Thank heavens it's over! I don't need to worry!

Oliver Jackson (10)
Thames View Junior School

SPARKLING CANDLE

It's sparkling, crackling and sizzling,
It's tough, mean and ferocious,
It's boiling, burning and scorching,
It's gloomy, embarrassed and emotional.

It's violent, powerful and mighty,
It's a dancer, wriggler and a cool dude,
It's vivid, bold and radiant,
It's miniature, micro but it feels gigantic.

It's miserable, lonely, lost its friends,
It's fierce, vicious and dangerous,
It's a snob, haughty and a show off,
It's friendly, wavy and it's a candle.

Mathew Price (9)
Thames View Junior School

THE PROUD CANDLE

So I slowly lit the candle spirit
I chose a fearless white snowy candle
And lit the careless spirit.
There's a spirit, a spirit with colours
It's the tallest, wavy spirit I've ever seen
Proud, determined, stunning, flickering
It's not a trapped spirit but a free spirit
The spirit started fading
It shrunk very slowly but noisily
I suddenly got miserable
I woke up with a sad feeling
The sparkling spirit had dissolved
The wax was like a tap
Dripping so slow but loud.

Samantha Richard (10)
Thames View Junior School

THE FLICKERING, FIERY FLAME

The flame flickered, proudly
The flame shimmered, quickly
Just like the fearless, jumpy fire
Who ferociously chases everyone!

The flame is blazing, brightly
The flame is fierce, evil
He emotionally dances and bounces
Waving up and down!

The flame is shallow, troubled
The flame is wavering, fast
Twisting, turning, swaying
Side to side!

Then the candle melts, slowly
Fading down and down
He doesn't feel like living
Any longer.

But then . . .

He feels proud, gleaming, sparkling and brilliant
He feels funny,
Slowly melting down
Now soft and slow
When there is no trace,
He's no longer living.

Katy Everett (9)
Thames View Junior School

MOVING OUT

Hello, I've just
been told to get out of my home,

I went to take,
a bear called Slate,

plus a ted
I really hate,

but now I've decided,
to take a mate,

and a cat that my
mum really hates,

plus a bed that
I like the best.

Sorry, now I've
got to go,
see you soon I hope.

David Trice (10)
Thames View Junior School